DENMARK 2016 HUMAN RIGHTS REPORT

EXECUTIVE SUMMARY

The Kingdom of Denmark is a constitutional monarchy with democratic, parliamentary rule. Queen Margrethe II is head of state. A prime minister, usually the leader of the majority party of a multiparty coalition, is head of government and presides over the cabinet, which is accountable to a unicameral parliament (Folketing). Greenland and the Faroe Islands are autonomous parts of the Kingdom of Denmark, with similar political structures and legal rights. They manage most of their domestic affairs, while the central Danish government is responsible for constitutional matters, citizenship, monetary and currency matters, foreign relations, and defense and security policy. National elections in June 2015, which observers deemed free and fair, resulted in a single-party minority government led by the center-right Liberal (Venstre) Party.

Civilian authorities maintained effective control over the security forces.

The main human rights problems concerned the treatment of irregular migrants from outside Europe. The law permits the government to seize migrants' jewelry and money upon entry into the country and restricts the ability of illegal migrants to appeal to the European Court of Human Rights (ECHR) and other international human rights entities. Human rights observers reported that irregular migrants were subject to protracted detention, poor housing conditions, isolation in confinement, travel restrictions, and restrictions on employment. There were reported cases of physical abuse at the Naestved Asylum Center, abuse of lesbian, gay, bisexual, transgender, and intersex (LGBTI) migrants, and forced prostitution of migrant boys at Sandholm Asylum Center.

Other problems included the occasional holding of detainees with convicts and children with adults, the excessive use of solitary and incommunicado detention, travel bans to certain countries, corruption in the awarding of government contracts, violence against women, child abuse, excessively long restraint of psychiatric patients, and discrimination against Muslims.

The government took steps to prosecute officials accused of committing abuses, whether in the military or elsewhere in government.

Section 1. Respect for the Integrity of the Person, Including Freedom from:

a. Arbitrary Deprivation of Life and other Unlawful or Politically Motivated Killings

There were no reports the government or its agents committed arbitrary or unlawful killings.

b. Disappearance

There were no reports of politically motivated disappearances.

c. Torture and Other Cruel, Inhuman, or Degrading Treatment or Punishment

The constitution and law prohibit such practices, and there were no reports government officials employed them. There were, however, reports of abuses at an asylum center in Naestved (see section 2.d.).

Prison and Detention Center Conditions

Prison and detention center conditions generally met international standards.

Physical Conditions: Women and men were held in the same institutions, but not in mixed-sex cells. According to human rights observers, authorities continued occasionally to hold pretrial detainees with convicted criminals and to detain children with adults. Human rights groups continued to criticize what they deemed authorities' excessive use of solitary confinement.

The nongovernmental organization (NGO) Danish Institute of Human Rights (DIHR) criticized detention center conditions for foreigners at Ellebaek Detention Center, including the detention of children, and called the health screening and language interpretation services there insufficient.

In 2015, the most recent period for which data was available, two prisoners committed suicide, and two died of natural causes in prisons and detention centers.

Independent Monitoring: The parliamentary ombudsman functioned as a prison ombudsman as required. The government additionally permitted monitoring visits by independent human rights observers, including media.

Independent observers, such as the Council of Europe's Committee for the Prevention of Torture, the International Committee of the Red Cross, and other independent observer NGOs, regularly received access to police headquarters, prisons, establishments for the detention of minors, asylum centers, and other detention facilities.

d. Arbitrary Arrest or Detention

The constitution and law prohibit arbitrary arrest and detention, and the government generally observed these prohibitions.

Role of the Police and Security Apparatus

The National Police maintain internal security, and the Danish Immigration Service manages immigration. The National Police are responsible for internal security. The National Police and the Immigration Service are responsible for border enforcement at the country's ports of entry as well as for the temporary border controls instituted to limit the flow of migrants from Germany.

The Armed Forces report to the Ministry of Defense and have responsibility for external security as well as some domestic security responsibilities, such as disaster response and maritime sovereignty enforcement. As of June the Home Guard, a volunteer militia without constabulary powers under the Ministry of Defense, assisted the National Police in conducting border checks.

Civilian authorities maintained effective control over the national police and the Danish Immigration Service, and the government has effective mechanisms to investigate and punish abuse and corruption. The Independent Police Complaints Authority received 509 complaints about police conduct in 2015.

Arrest Procedures and Treatment of Detainees

The law allows police to begin investigations and make arrests either on their own initiative based upon visual evidence or based on a court order following an indictment filed with the courts by public prosecutors.

The law mandates that Danish citizens and legal migrants taken into custody appear before a judge within 24 hours. The law requires police to make every effort to limit post-arrest detention time to less than 12 hours; statistics on the actual time between the detention of a person and the detainee's first appearance before a judge were not available. There are generally no limitations to prompt access to counsel. Authorities may hold irregular migrants up to 72 hours before bringing them before a judge or releasing them. In most cases authorities may not hold irregular migrants for more than 72 hours while the judge determines their status. Under new rules put in place in November 2015, authorities may detain asylum seekers to determine their identity and the basis for their application. In addition, the Ministry of Integration, Immigration, and Housing may temporarily suspend the requirement of a 72-hour case review if the inflow of requests for asylum is determined to be too high to be completed within 72 hours.

Authorities generally respected the right of detainees to a prompt judicial determination and informed them promptly of charges against them. There is no bail system; judges decide either to release detainees on their own recognizance or to keep them in detention until trial. A judge may authorize detention prior to trial only when authorities are charging the detainee with a violation that could result in a prison sentence of more than 18 months or when the judge determines the detainee would seek to impede the investigation of the case, would be a flight risk, or is likely to commit a new offense. The standard period of pretrial custody is up to four weeks, but a court order may further extend custody in four-week increments.

Arrested persons have the right to unsupervised visits with an attorney from the time police bring them to a police station. There was, however, no information to indicate that police changed their long-standing practice of frequently denying such access until the defendant appeared in court for a remand hearing. The government provides counsel for those who could not afford legal representation. Detainees have the right to inform their next of kin of their arrest, although authorities may deny this right if information about the detention could compromise the police investigation. Detainees have the right to obtain medical treatment, and authorities generally respected this right. Police may deny other forms of visitation, subject to a court appeal, but generally did not do so. While there were no known instances of authorities' holding suspects incommunicado or placing them under house arrest, human rights observers expressed concern about the administrative use of solitary confinement in some cases, as well as a need to reduce the use and duration of remand custody while waiting for trial.

<u>Detainee's Ability to Challenge Lawfulness of Detention before a Court</u>: A detainee has the right to challenge the lawfulness of his or her detention at an initial hearing and to have a review by both the district court and the high court. Both the detainee and prosecutor can appeal the district court's decision on

detention or release to the high court. An appeal can also be made after the hearing by sending a letter or e-mail to the court that made the decision within 14 days of the hearing, and in cases of imprisonment the detainee can request the prison warden to notify the court. If the defendant is acquitted after being taken into custody, or if the prosecution withdraws its charges, the former detainee may apply for financial compensation. The claim, however, must be filed within two months of the final case judgment in order to receive compensation.

Protracted Detention of Rejected Asylum Seekers or Stateless Persons: Authorities detained some unsuccessful applicants for asylum pending deportation. Human rights observers continued to express concern that authorities could imprison vulnerable persons, including victims of torture, mentally ill individuals, and minors, pending the finalization of their cases. These observers stated that unaccompanied minors from Afghanistan whose asylum applications had been rejected were held in detention together with criminals. The DIHR further alleged that health screenings and resources for detained children at the Ellebaek Detention Center were insufficient.

e. Denial of Fair Public Trial

The constitution and law provide for an independent judiciary, and the government generally respected judicial independence.

Trial Procedures

The constitution provides for the right to a fair, public trial, and an independent judiciary generally enforced this right.

Defendants enjoy the right to a presumption of innocence; a prompt and detailed notification of the charges against them (with free interpretation as necessary); a fair and public trial without undue delay; be present at their trial; communicate with an attorney of their choice (or have one provided at public expense if unable to pay); have adequate time and facilities to prepare a defense; free interpretation as necessary from the moment charged through all appeals; have access to government-held evidence; confront prosecution or plaintiff witnesses and present one's own witnesses and evidence; not to be compelled to testify or confess guilt; and appeal one's case. The constitution and law extend these rights to all citizens and legal residents.

Several human rights groups have protested a law adopted in March that introduced new conditions for applicants seeking to appeal cases to international human rights appeals bodies. The law now requires that the appellant should have "reasonable grounds" to submit an appeal. Human rights groups asserted the law unjustly targeted asylum seekers, who as a group have fewer legal appeal channels than citizens or legal residents.

Political Prisoners and Detainees

There were no reports of political prisoners or detainees.

Civil Judicial Procedures and Remedies

Individuals or organizations may bring civil lawsuits seeking damages for a human rights violation. The complainant may also pursue an administrative resolution. Persons may appeal court decisions involving alleged violations of the European Convention on Human Rights to the ECHR after they exhaust all avenues of appeal in national courts.

f. Arbitrary or Unlawful Interference with Privacy, Family, Home, or Correspondence

The constitution and law prohibit such actions, and there were no reports the government failed to respect these prohibitions.

In December 2015 parliament adopted a bill that allows the Defense Intelligence Service to intercept communications of both citizens and foreigners abroad if there are reasons to believe that they are participating in terrorist-related activities or threats to the country's interests. A court order is required before the intercept begins.

Section 2. Respect for Civil Liberties, Including:

a. Freedom of Speech and Press

The constitution and law provide for freedom of speech and press, and the government generally respected these rights. An independent press, an effective judiciary, and a functioning democratic political system combined to promote freedom of speech and press.

<u>Freedom of Speech and Expression</u>: The law prohibits any public speech or the dissemination of statements or other pronouncements that threaten, deride, or degrade a group because of gender, race, skin color, national or ethnic background, religion, or sexual orientation. Authorities may fine or imprison offenders for up to two years. During the year there were two convictions for hate speech. One case involved the conviction of a council member from the Danish People's Party for tweeting anti-Semitic and anti-Muslim remarks. He was fined 8,000 kroner ($1,200). A second person was fined 1,600 kroner ($240) for spreading anti-Muslim statements on Facebook.

The law also prohibits blasphemy and provides that a person who publicly mocks or insults a legally existing religious community's tenets of faith or worship may be fined or imprisoned for up to four months. The government has not prosecuted a blasphemy case since 1938.

<u>Press and Media Freedoms</u>: Independent media were active and expressed a wide variety of views without restriction.

In June an appeals court affirmed that two former employees of Roj TV were guilty of channeling 33.5 million kroner ($5 million) to the PKK. In 2014 the Supreme Court revoked the broadcasting license of the Denmark-based Kurdish television channel Roj TV for promoting the activities of the terrorist Kurdistan Workers Party (PKK) and for receiving support from the PKK. The court fined the station 10 million kroner ($1.5 million), after which it went into bankruptcy.

Internet Freedom

The government did not restrict or disrupt access to the internet or censor online content, and there were no credible reports that the government monitored private online communications without appropriate legal authority. Internet service providers continued to employ internet filters designed to block child pornography and websites hosting copyright-infringed material. There were no reports of the filter's affecting legitimate websites.

According to 2015 statistics compiled by the International Telecommunication Union, 43 percent of the population in Denmark had a fixed broadband subscription, compared with 36 percent in the Faroe Islands and 17 percent in Greenland. According to the same source, 96 percent of the population in Denmark were internet users, compared with 94 percent in the Faroe Islands and 68 percent in Greenland.

Academic Freedom and Cultural Events

There were no government restrictions on academic freedom or cultural events.

b. Freedom of Peaceful Assembly and Association

The constitution provides for the freedoms of assembly and association, and the government generally respected these rights.

c. Freedom of Religion

See the Department of State's *International Religious Freedom Report* at www.state.gov/religiousfreedomreport/.

d. Freedom of Movement, Internally Displaced Persons, Protection of Refugees, and Stateless Persons

The constitution and law provide for freedom of internal movement, foreign travel, emigration, and repatriation, and the government generally respected these rights.

Abuse of Migrants, Refugees, and Stateless Persons: According to Amnesty International, individuals awaiting the result of their asylum claim or deportation to their country of origin, including victims of torture, unaccompanied children, and persons with mental illness, continued to be held in detention for immigration control purposes. No effective screening of asylum seekers was put in place to identify individuals who were unfit to be placed in detention.

There were reports of abuses at an asylum center in the Naestved Asylum Center, where the camp manager was filmed using excessive force against one of the camp residents. According to Amnesty Denmark and media sources, residents lived in fear because the manager threatened residents, confiscated telephones, and warned he would adversely influence their asylum cases. In light of the allegations, Langeland Municipality dismissed the manager in May.

According to LGBT Asylum, there were at least 10 cases of verbal threats or physical abuse reported against LGBTI asylum seekers residing in group lodging in asylum centers across the country when their sexual identity was discovered by other residents.

Staff at the Sandholm Asylum Center raised concerns that groups of teenage boys residing in the center were being coerced into prostitution. Sandholm staff reported several specific cases where boys reported sexual abuse as well as suspicious signs of abuse. Since the typical length of stay at Sandholm was approximately three months, it was difficult for staff and local authorities to investigate the cases, since by the time evidence of abuse surfaced, the victims had moved on to other asylum centers around the country.

The law permits the detention of asylum seekers by the National Police for the purposes of registration. It authorizes the National Police to suspend the time limit for asylum seekers' right to judicial review of detention within 72 hours of processing an asylum applicant. At times the processing can take as long as two weeks depending on the number of cases. Human rights observers continued to express concern that authorities could imprison vulnerable persons, including victims of torture, mentally ill individuals, and minors, pending the finalization of their cases.

In February the parliamentary ombudsman, along with domestic NGOs, made an unannounced visit to the asylum center in Vridsloselille, where foreigners due to leave the country are held with foreigners with pending asylum cases who are detained in order to ensure their continued presence. The ombudsman expressed serious concern about the conditions at the facility, including lack of information, communication, and human contact for many of the residents. The ombudsman further criticized the absence of screening for torture and the risk of suicide. In addition, the DIHR criticized the detention and deportation center conditions for poor language interpretation services and health screening at facilities for asylum seekers.

The government cooperated with the Office of the UN High Commissioner for Refugees (UNHCR) and other humanitarian organizations in providing protection and assistance to refugees, asylum seekers, stateless persons, and other persons of concern.

<u>Foreign Travel</u>: Changes to the passport law in March and to the penal code in July give police the right to seize the passports and impose travel bans on citizens suspected of planning to travel abroad with the intention of participating in activities that may be a danger to the country's national security. The legal changes also prohibit citizens and foreigners residing in the country from travelling to conflict zones where terror organizations are part of the conflict. Travel to these areas now requires prior approval by authorities, and those who fail to receive

approval face penalties of up to six years in prison. Observers criticized the law for being vague as to the areas where travel is prohibited and the sides of a conflict to which the prohibition applies.

In June a judge in the Copenhagen City Court approved the confiscation of a citizen's passport and imposed a travel ban against her after she returned to the country from the Kurdish areas in Iraq and Syria, where she fought with the women's branch of the Kurdish People's Protection Units in Syria and Iraq against Daesh.

Protection of Refugees

<u>Access to Asylum</u>: The law provides for the granting of asylum and refugee status, and the government has established a system for providing protection to refugees.

On January 26, the government approved and implemented controversial immigration legislation, popularly known in international media as the "jewelry law." The law greatly tightens immigration policy and aims to dissuade asylum seekers from choosing the country as a destination. It authorizes the government to seize cash and valuables, excluding items of sentimental value, with a value greater than 10,000 kroner ($1,500) in order to reimburse the government for costs incurred in providing emergency services including food, lodging, and other benefits to refugees and asylum seekers who become the country's responsibility once they are within its borders. The law also seeks to align more closely the criteria for support given asylum seekers with those of citizens receiving social assistance for whom a much higher minimum threshold exists. The law also extends timelines for family reunification cases (up to three years instead of one year) as well as the minimum period to obtain a permanent residence permit from five years to six years.

According to statistics from the Danish Immigration Service, 18,943 asylum seekers received residence permits in the country in 2015. This was a significant increase from 2014, when the country granted 8,506 asylum seekers residence permits.

<u>Safe Country of Origin/Transit</u>: The government employs the EU's Dublin III Regulation, which permits authorities to turn back or deport individuals who attempt to enter the country through a "safe country of origin and transit" or were previously registered in another Dublin Regulation country. In addition to other EU countries, the government considers Albania, Bosnia and Herzegovina,

Macedonia, Kosovo, Montenegro, Serbia, Norway, Iceland, Switzerland, Liechtenstein, Moldova, Russia, Canada, the United States, Mongolia, Australia, Japan, and New Zealand to be safe countries of origin.

In September 2015 the government partially suspended the Dublin Regulation for migrants wishing to continue to other Nordic countries, who were allowed to transit the country without registering. After Sweden introduced identification checks at the Danish border in January to prevent undocumented migrants from entering Sweden, the government reintroduced border controls on the German border in January in order to avoid an accumulation of irregular migrants attempting to transit to Sweden.

Freedom of movement: The government placed asylum seekers in camps or centers where there were no restrictions on movement while the asylum seeker resided within the asylum center system. Once an asylum seeker was granted refugee status and residency, however, the individual had to reside in the designated municipality regardless of his or her place of employment. The refugee was required to remain in that municipality for at least three years and to forego all benefits if he or she decided to move.

Employment: Although asylum seekers received a stipend while they resided within the asylum center system, they were effectively prevented from working by rules limiting them to one or two weeks of work per year. Furthermore, refugees granted residency who wished to start their own private business had to forego all government social benefits upon establishing the business.

Durable Solutions: The government has a flexible three-year quota-based national resettlement program, which is run in coordination with UNHCR. In 2015 the country received 580 UNHCR refugees. The government helped facilitate local integration with an array of social services and specific programs targeted at integrating newcomers.

Temporary Protection: The government also provided temporary protection to individuals who may not qualify as refugees, and provided it to 1,068 persons in 2015.

Stateless Persons

According to UNHCR statistics, 6,580 stateless persons lived in the country as of December 2015, the latest date for which statistics were available. According to

Statistics Denmark and the Ministry of Immigration, Integration, and Housing, 1,734 stateless persons sought asylum in the country in 2015. Citizenship is based primarily on the citizenship of one's parents. Stateless persons born outside the country to noncitizens, including refugees, are not eligible to acquire citizenship but may acquire residency permits. Certain persons born in the country to noncitizens may acquire citizenship by virtue of UN conventions to which the government is a signatory. This is not an automatic process, and in most cases such individuals must apply for citizenship before their 21st birthday.

Section 3. Freedom to Participate in the Political Process

The constitution and laws provide citizens, including those of Greenland and the Faroe Islands, the ability to choose their government in free and fair periodic elections held by secret ballot and based on universal and equal suffrage.

Elections and Political Participation

Recent Elections: The country held free and fair parliamentary elections in June 2015. There were no reports of abuses or electoral irregularities. The Faroe Islands held parliamentary elections in September 2015, and Greenland did so in 2014. These elections were also considered to be free and fair.

Participation of Women and Minorities: There were no laws limiting the participation of women and members of minorities in the political process, and they did participate.

Section 4. Corruption and Lack of Transparency in Government

The law provides criminal penalties for corruption by officials, and the government generally implemented the law effectively. There were two reported cases of corruption during the year.

Corruption: After filing charges against 13 persons in connection with a bribery investigation of information technology (IT) service contracts for the Zealand region in 2015, the government prosecutor for serious economic and international crime charged an additional 27 officials in June. According to the prosecutor, the officials, all IT employees, allegedly received gifts of electronic devices from a company involved in providing electronic services to various public institutions, including the Foreign Ministry, the National Police, the Public Prosecutor's Office, the Copenhagen Council, the national railway corporation, and the Prison Service.

The judge advocate general was investigating the allegations of corruption in relation to employees at the Ministry of Defense and the Defense Intelligence Service.

According to media and Siumut Party officials, former Greenlandic premier and current member of the Danish parliament Aleqa Hammond was expelled from the Siumut Party on August 24, after revelations she misused her parliamentary credit card by making private purchases. Hammond retained her seat in parliament as an independent member.

Financial Disclosure: The law does not require public officials to disclose their personal finances. Government officials may not work on specific matters in which they, persons they represent, or persons with whom they have close relations have a personal or economic interest. Officials must inform their superiors of any possible conflicts of interest that might disqualify them.

Public Access to Information: The law provides for public access to government information, and the government effectively implemented the law and granted access to citizens and noncitizens, including foreign media. The law provides for an appeals process. The law exempts from freedom of information requests documents involving advice provided to ministers by civil servants.

Section 5. Governmental Attitude Regarding International and Nongovernmental Investigation of Alleged Violations of Human Rights

A variety of domestic and international human rights groups generally operated without government restriction, investigating and publishing their findings on human rights cases. Government officials often were cooperative and responsive to their views.

Government Human Rights Bodies: The parliamentary ombudsman investigated complaints regarding national and local public authorities and any decisions they made regarding the treatment of citizens and their cases. The ombudsman can independently inspect prisons, detention centers, and psychiatric hospitals. An ombudsman for European matters oversaw compliance with EU basic rights, a consumers' ombudsman investigated complaints related to discriminatory marketing, and two royal ombudsmen represented the government in the Faroe Islands and Greenland. These ombudsmen enjoyed the government's cooperation, operated without government or political interference, had adequate resources, and were considered effective.

Section 6. Discrimination, Societal Abuses, and Trafficking in Persons

Women

Rape and Domestic Violence: The law criminalizes rape, including spousal rape, and domestic violence. Penalties for rape include imprisonment for eight years and up to 12 years in cases where the rape was considered violent and dangerous in nature, or if there were other aggravating circumstances. The government effectively prosecuted persons accused of rape. According to National Police and Ministry of Justice statistics, there were 628 reports of rape in 2015 compared with 462 reported cases in 2014.

Faroese law criminalizes rape, but considers nonconsensual sex with a victim in a "helpless state" to be sexual abuse rather than rape and stipulates a much lighter penalty for such acts. In certain instances it also reduces the level of penalty for rape and sexual violence within marriage or provides for exclusion of punishment altogether. The penalties for rape include imprisonment for eight years and up to 12 years in cases where the rape was considered violent and dangerous in nature, or if there were other aggravating circumstances. "Mitigating circumstances" such as marriage can in some cases reduce imprisonment to four years. According to National Police statistics, there were 26 reports of crimes against sexual morality, including rape and indecent exposure in 2015, compared with 25 cases in 2014.

Greenlandic law criminalizes rape but reduces the penalty for rape and sexual violence within marriage. There are no fixed imprisonment terms for rape, because the Greenlandic criminal justice system utilizes an offender treatment model based on traditional indigenous practices that gives courts a great deal of flexibility in sentencing. Persons convicted of rape typically receive a prison sentence of one-and-a-half years. According to National Police reports, there were 134 reports of rape in 2015, compared with 132 reports of rape in 2014.

The crime of rape was widely believed to be underreported throughout the kingdom. A study done in 2014 by Copenhagen University in conjunction with the Ministry of Justice and the National Police estimated that approximately 3,600 rapes occurred in the country, rather than the 462 reported that year. According to the Ministry of Justice, the average penalty for rape was two years of prison, which many observers criticized as far too low.

Violence against women, including spousal abuse, remained a societal problem. A 2015 report by the Mary Foundation found that 62 percent of Greenlandic women experienced violence at least once in their lifetime. Domestic violence was also considered a social taboo and was alleged to be underreported, particularly in many small, tightly knit Greenlandic communities.

The government and NGOs operated 24-hour hotlines, counseling centers, and shelters for female survivors of violence. The royal family supported a variety of NGOs that worked to improve conditions and services at shelters and to assist families afflicted with domestic violence.

Sexual Harassment: The law prohibits sexual harassment and provides that authorities may order a perpetrator or an employer who allowed or failed to prevent an incident of harassment to pay monetary compensation to victims. The government enforced the law effectively. The law provides that most such cases be processed through the labor unions, which function as civil society organizations, or the Equal Treatment Board.

The DIHR highlighted that instances of sexual harassment were significantly underreported. According to a 2014 report from the EU's Agency for Fundamental Rights, the latest available, 37 percent of all Danish women reported experiencing sexual harassment. In October 2015 the government reprioritized 6.5 million kroner ($975,000) for projects designed to support victims of harassment and stalking.

During the year the Danish Economic Council of the Labor Movement reported that one in four women had experienced sexual harassment, threats of violence, or bullying at work over the previous year. The report also indicated that many hesitated to come forward with complaints due to workplace cultures or concern their complaint would be dismissed.

Reproductive Rights: Couples and individuals have the right to decide the number, spacing, and timing of their children; manage their reproductive health; and have access to the information and means to do so, free from discrimination, coercion, or violence.

Discrimination: Women have the same legal status and rights as men, including under family, labor, property, nationality, and inheritance laws. There was little discrimination reported in employment, ownership and management of businesses, or access to credit, education, or housing.

Children

<u>Birth Registration</u>: Most children acquire citizenship from their parents. Stateless persons and certain persons born in the country to noncitizens may acquire citizenship by naturalization, provided, in most cases, that they apply for citizenship before their 21st birthday. The law requires that medical practitioners promptly register the births of children they deliver, and they generally did so.

<u>Child Abuse</u>: The National Police and Public Prosecutor's Office actively investigated child abuse cases. In 2015 authorities prosecuted 146 allegations of rape involving a child 12 years and younger and 156 allegations of sexual intercourse with a child 15 years and younger.

In Greenland child abuse and neglect remained a significant problem. According to an April 2015 study by the Danish National Center for Social Research commissioned by the Greenlandic government, every other woman and every third man indicated that they were subject to sexual contact with an adult before they turned 15 years of age. Of the sample, 7 percent indicated their first sexual contact occurred before they had turned seven years of age. According to the Greenlandic branch of the DIHR, approximately 5,000 Greenlandic children did not thrive due to sexual and physical abuse or negligence by parents who were suffering from alcohol abuse as well as a lack of economic, personal, and social opportunities. National Police statistics from 2015, reported 31 prosecutions for sexual intercourse with a child who was 15 years of age or younger and nine cases of sexual intercourse with a child who was 16 or 17.

<u>Early and Forced Marriage</u>: The legal age for marriage is 18.

<u>Sexual Exploitation of Children</u>: The law prohibits the commercial sexual exploitation of children and child pornography. The government generally enforced these laws. In 2015 authorities prosecuted 110 cases of child pornography, up from 71 cases in 2014, perhaps due to changes in statistical methods. The minimum age of consensual sexual activity is 15. The purchase of sexual services from a person under the age of 18 is illegal.

<u>Displaced Children</u>: The government regarded refugees and migrants who were unaccompanied minors as vulnerable, and the law includes special rules regarding them. A personal representative is appointed for all unaccompanied children who seek asylum or who stay in the country without permission. The powers and

obligations of a personal representative are equal to those of a holder of custody rights. The representative supports and cares for the minor and also attends asylum interviews or other meetings with authorities.

According to the DIHR, displaced children performed less successfully than other children in almost all areas, including schooling, health, and general well-being. Children placed outside their home, especially children who are placed at a later stage in their lives, continued to run much greater risk of not completing secondary education or receiving higher education.

<u>International Child Abductions</u>: The country is a party to the 1980 Hague Convention on the Civil Aspects of International Child Abduction. See the Department of State's *Annual Report on International Parental Child Abduction* at travel.state.gov/content/childabduction/en/legal/compliance.html.

Anti-Semitism

The Jewish NGO community in Denmark estimated the Jewish population at between 6,000 and 8,000 persons.

In January a 16-year-old girl was arrested after police found bomb manuals and chemicals for making explosives at her residence. In March the girl was charged with preparing a terrorist attack against the Jewish private school in Copenhagen as well as another school. In addition, her friend, a 24-year-old who had recently returned from fighting in Syria, was arrested for acquiring bomb-making materials and plotting attacks on two additional schools. At year's end both individuals were in custody and awaiting their final hearing.

In February a council member from the Danish People's Party, Mogens Camre, was fined 8,000 kroner ($1,200) for tweeting anti-Semitic and anti-Muslim remarks.

Concerns remained in the Jewish community regarding a growing movement to prohibit infant male circumcision. Some organizations and individuals, including members of parliament, continued to campaign to have the practice banned.

Trafficking in Persons

See the Department of State's *Trafficking in Persons Report* at www.state.gov/j/tip/rls/tiprpt/.

Persons with Disabilities

The law prohibits discrimination against persons with physical, sensory, intellectual, and mental disabilities in employment, education, air travel and other transportation, access to health care, the judicial system, and the provision of other government services. It also mandates access by persons with disabilities to government buildings, education, information, and communications. The government generally enforced these provisions. The DIHR reported that the enforcement of antidiscrimination laws was well established for the workplace but less so in other areas, such as laws on accessibility, coercive measures in psychiatric treatment, self-determination, political participation, inclusion in the labor market, and equal access to healthcare. In addition, outside the labor market persons with disabilities did not enjoy full legal protection against discrimination, because there is no express prohibition of discrimination against persons with disabilities and no duty on the part of service providers to make reasonable accommodations for persons with disabilities.

According to the DIHR's human rights status report for 2016, between 37 percent and 48 percent of persons with major physical or mental disabilities reported instances of discrimination. The parliamentary ombudsman monitored the treatment of persons with disabilities and issued opinions regarding complaints of disability discrimination.

In its 2016 human rights status report, the DIHR criticized the September 2015 amendment of the Mental Health Act for failing to end the use of physical restraints during psychiatric treatment for periods in excess of 48 hours. The DIHR reported that the proportion of adults subjected to coercion in psychiatry remained unchanged at more than 22 percent.

The right of persons with disabilities to vote or participate in civic affairs was generally not restricted, but some persons with disabilities reported problems in connection with elections, including ballots that were not accessible to blind persons or persons with learning disabilities. The country maintained a system of guardianship for persons considered incapable of managing their own affairs due to psychosocial or intellectual disabilities.

In April parliament amended the voting law to give those under guardianship, who do not possess legal capacity, the right to vote in local and regional elections, as well as elections to the European Parliament.

According to the Greenlandic branch of the DIHR, persons with disabilities in Greenland, including children, had limited access to support, including physical aids, counselling, educated professionals, and appropriate housing. In addition, some persons with severe disabilities were placed in foster homes far away from their families or relocated to foster homes in Denmark because of lack of resources in Greenland.

In the Faroe Islands, steps have been taken to ensure an inclusive education system that provides education for all young persons. The law allows upper secondary education for autistic persons.

National/Racial/Ethnic Minorities

According to the 2015 *Annual Report on Hate Crimes* published by the National Police, authorities recorded 198 hate crimes. The report categorized 104 of the hate crimes as racially motivated and three as having unspecified motivations. The government effectively investigated hate crimes and prosecuted the perpetrators.

Indigenous People

The law protects the rights of the indigenous Inuit inhabitants of Greenland, whose legal system seeks to accommodate their traditions. Through their elected internally autonomous government, they participated in decisions affecting their lands, culture, and traditions and the exploitation of energy, minerals, and other natural resources.

Indigenous Greenlandic people in Denmark remained underrepresented in the workforce, overrepresented on welfare rolls, and more susceptible to suicide, poverty, chronic health conditions, and sexual violence.

Acts of Violence, Discrimination, and Other Abuses Based on Sexual Orientation and Gender Identity

The law prohibits discrimination against persons based on sexual orientation. Any person who makes a statement or imparts other information that threatens, scorns, or degrades a group of persons because of their sexual orientation is liable to a fine or to imprisonment for not more than two years. If a person is found guilty of a crime the motive of which was the sexual orientation of the victim, the judge must consider that motive to be an aggravating factor when determining the sentence.

The law allows transgender persons to obtain official documents reflecting their new gender identity without requiring a diagnosis for a mental disorder or undergoing surgery.

According to the 2015 *Annual Report on Hate Crimes*, there were 31 incidents of hate crimes based on sexual orientation. Authorities actively investigated and punished those complicit in abuses.

In May parliament adopted a law to stop officially classifying transgender persons as having a mental or behavioral disorder. Guidelines published in 2015, however, preclude regular doctors from prescribing hormones for gender-reassignment, and as a result all transsexual individuals must now visit a single hospital in Copenhagen. Activists pointed to this policy, among other medical treatment options, as evidence of continuing discrimination against LGBTI individuals.

Other Societal Violence or Discrimination

In February the national television network TV2, a publicly owned broadcaster with an independent editorial board, aired a four-part investigative documentary that negatively depicted Islam in the country. The program used undercover and sensational videography that purported to show imams at eight well known conservative Sunni mosques encouraging behavior that violated social norms and, in some cases, the law. Academics and civil society criticized the series as over-simplifying and sensationalizing the attitudes of Muslims and further fueling national tensions over the integration of refugees and migrants.

In May, two Muslim girls were attacked when they walked past a bar in Odense. Three ethnic Danes started yelling racist comments at the two women. This quickly escalated into an argument and violence with one of the women's headscarves being ripped off. The woman later stated to the press that no onlookers attempted to stop the altercation.

In May the Center for Adult Education in Lyngby prohibited six Muslim women from wearing the niqab in school and referred them to their e-learning service. The school argued that the niqab limited interaction between teacher and student. Minister of Education Ellen Trane Norby supported the decision on the grounds the education center is an independent entity as well as the school's argument that student-teacher interaction is important to the learning experience. Adult education centers in Aarhus, Albertslund, and Copenhagen also previously prohibited niqabs.

According to the 2015 *Annual Report on Hate Crimes*, authorities recorded 60 hate crimes as religiously motivated.

Section 7. Worker Rights

a. Freedom of Association and the Right to Collective Bargaining

The law states all workers may form or join independent unions of their choosing without previous authorization or excessive requirements. The law provides for the right to collective bargaining and to legal strikes but does not provide nonresident foreign workers on Danish ships the right to participate in the country's collective bargaining agreements. It allows unions to conduct their activities without interference and prohibits antiunion discrimination. Workers fired for union activities can take the employer to court and receive reinstatement or a cash settlement on a case-by-case basis. These laws were effectively enforced. Resources, inspections, and remediation including supporting regulations were adequate. Penalties were sufficient to deter violations. Breaches of collective agreement are typically referred to the Labor Court, and if the parties agree the industrial arbitration courts may decide whether there was a breach. Penalties for violation are determined on the basis of the facts of the case and with due regard to the degree that the breach of agreement was excusable. Penalties typically imposed by the Labor Court frequently amount to 500,000 kroner ($75,000) and in more serious cases as high as 20 million kroner ($3 million). Lengthy judicial delays and appeals did not seriously hamper enforcement.

Employers and the government generally respected freedom of association and the right to collective bargaining. Annual collective bargaining agreements covered members of the workforce associated with unions and indirectly affected the wages and working conditions of nonunion employees.

b. Prohibition of Forced or Compulsory Labor

The law prohibits all forms of forced or compulsory labor, including by children, and the government effectively enforced this prohibition. The law prescribes sanctions of up to 10 years' imprisonment for violations and was generally sufficient to deter violations. In 2015 authorities identified 44 victims, 43 of whom were forced to commit crimes and one who was forced to provide labor. The government also trained tax inspectors and trade union officials to identify forced labor.

Also see the Department of State's *Trafficking in Persons Report* at
www.state.gov/j/tip/rls/tiprpt/.

c. Prohibition of Child Labor and Minimum Age for Employment

The minimum legal age for full-time employment is 15. The law sets a minimum
age of 13 for part-time employment and limits school-age children to less
strenuous tasks. The law limits work hours and sets occupational health and safety
restrictions for children, and the government effectively enforced these laws.
Minors are not permitted to operate heavy machinery or handle toxic substances,
including harsh detergents. Minors may only carry out "light work," which is the
equivalent of lifting no more than 26.4 pounds from the ground and 52.8 pounds
from waist-height. For minors working in jobs where there is a higher risk of
robbery or if the minor works in a snack bar, kiosk, bakery, gas station, or any
other location where there are customers, a coworker over the age of 18 must
always be present between the hours of 6:00 p.m. and 6:00 a.m. on weekdays, and
2:00 p.m. and 6:00 a.m. on weekends.

The law prohibits the exploitation of children in the workplace, and the
government, through the Danish Working Environment Authority (DWEA),
enforced this prohibition effectively. Information regarding resources,
investigations, and remediation efforts was not available because there were no
reported instances of unlawful child labor. Penalties for violations are determined
based upon the size of the company and the seriousness of the violation. They
range from fines between 40,000 to 80,000 kroner ($6,000 to $12,000) and two
years' imprisonment.

d. Discrimination with Respect to Employment and Occupation

The law prohibits employment discrimination with respect to race, color, sex,
religion, political opinion, national origin or citizenship, social origin, disability,
sexual orientation or gender identity, age, language, HIV-positive status, or other
communicable diseases. The government generally enforced these laws
effectively. Penalties for violations include fines of between 5,000 to 10,000
kroner ($750 to $1,500) or imprisonment of up to two years and were generally
sufficient to deter violations. Discrimination in employment and occupation was
limited and occurred with respect to gender and ethnicity (see section 6).

The law requires the 1,100 largest companies to establish targets for the participation of women on their boards, develop specific plans for recruiting women, and describe their actions to promote women's participation in annual reports that explain why any targets were not met.

Greenland prohibits gender discrimination. There are no laws protecting against discrimination based on race, ethnic origin, religion, sexual orientation, or disability. Gender discrimination is prohibited by a law that also establishes the Council of Gender Equality in Greenland. Danish gender equality law does not apply to Greenland. The mandate of the Council of Gender Equality in Greenland includes examining, on its own initiative or by request, measures relating to gender equality. In all cases of discrimination, no national complaints procedure for individuals exists other than taking a case to court or when dealing with a public authority to refer the case to the parliamentary ombudsman.

e. Acceptable Conditions of Work

The law does not mandate a national minimum wage, and unions and employer associations negotiated minimum wages in collective bargaining agreements. The average minimum wage for all private and public sector collective bargaining agreements was 110 kroner ($16.50) per hour, exclusive of pension benefits. The law requires equal pay for equal work; migrant workers are entitled to the same minimum wages and working conditions as other workers.

Workers generally worked a 37.5-hour week established by contract rather than law. Workers received premium pay for overtime, and there was no compulsory overtime. Working hours were determined by collective bargaining agreements adhering to the EU directive that an average workweek not exceed 48 hours. These agreements also provided workers at least five weeks' paid vacation per year.

The law prescribes conditions of work, including safety and health standards, and authorities enforced compliance with labor legislation. Minimum wage, hours of work, and occupational, safety, and health (OSH) standards were effectively enforced in all sectors, including the informal economy. Penalties for OSH violations, for both employees and employers, include fines or imprisonment of up to one year. The penalty may be increased by two years if the violation resulted in a serious personal injury or death. In specific cases of OSH violations that are subject to only fines, the Minister for Employment may lay down regulations on how the DWEA may, in the notification of a fine, declare that the case may be settled out of court. These penalties were considered sufficient to deter violations.

The Ministry of Employment is responsible for the framework and rules regarding working conditions, health and safety, industrial injuries, financial support, and disability allowances, as well as enterprise placement services. The DWEA is the agency under the Ministry of Employment responsible for enforcing health and safety rules and regulations. This is carried out through inspection visits as well as guidance to companies and their internal safety organizations. The DWEA's scope applies to all industrial sectors except for work carried out in the employer's private household, work carried out exclusively by members of the employer's family, and work carried out by military personnel. In certain sectors regulation and enforcement has been devolved to other authorities: the Danish Energy Agency is responsible for supervision of offshore installations, the Maritime Authority is responsible for supervision of shipping, and the Civil Aviation Administration is responsible for supervision in the aviation sector.

The DWEA has authority to report violations to the police or the courts if an employer fails to make required improvements by the deadline set by the DWEA. Court decisions regarding violations were released to the public and show past fines of 2,500 kroner ($375) to 40,000 kroner ($6,000) imposed against noncompliant companies or court-ordered reinstatement of employment. Greenland and the Faroe Islands had similar work conditions, except in both cases collective bargaining agreements set the standard workweek at 40 hours.

Workers can remove themselves from situations they believe endanger their health or safety without jeopardy to their employment, and authorities effectively protected employees in these situations. The same laws protect legal immigrants and foreign workers and apply equally to both categories of workers.

In 2015 the DWEA employed approximately 600 OSH inspectors and staff who carried out 17,391 workplace inspections. The number of labor inspectors was considered sufficient to enforce compliance. The DWEA effectively enforced labor health and safety standards in all sectors, including enforcement of limiting the hours worked per week.

Vulnerable groups generally include migrant and seasonal laborers, as well as young workers.

In January the DWEA increased monitoring of companies found with serious infractions through closer supervision of the company's work and labor practices as well as improved dialogue with the company's employees and supervisors in order to eliminate OSH risks. In the lead-up to the summer fruit harvest season, the DWEA, in coordination with the National Police and the tax authority (SKAT), increased inspections of fruit and vegetable farms that typically rely on seasonal foreign labor to ensure that labor and tax laws were being followed. This was the fourth season that the DWEA carried out such joint action. In 2015 there were 61 joint agricultural inspections, while in 2014 there were 47 joint inspections. The DWEA also increased inspections in the construction, agriculture, forestry, and fishery sectors, the sectors with the highest OSH violations. In 2015 the DWEA carried out inspections in 1,980 businesses in the agriculture, forestry, and fishery sectors, while in 2014 the DWEA inspected 1,945 businesses. In 2015 the DWEA also inspected 2,188 construction sector businesses, while in 2014 it inspected 1,924 businesses. In July the DWEA established a hazardous substances hotline where workers can call in with questions on the proper handling and regulations for working with epoxies, isocyanates, as well as other carcinogenic and allergenic chemicals.

As part of an EU-funded project, the Center for Human Trafficking in coordination with the DWEA identified risk factors related to human trafficking in the hotel sector and developed and publicized guidelines for the hospitality sector to assist employers prevent labor exploitation. SKAT and the DWEA have carried out training of inspectors to identify possible labor trafficking victims based on working conditions.

The majority of informal work occurs in restaurants, hotels, and household cleaning services, as well as with seasonal agricultural workers. There have been growing concerns in media and rights groups regarding the exploitation of au pairs, since under labor laws au pair work is considered work carried out in the employer's private household. According to Immigration Service statistics, 1,624 au pairs were granted visas in 2015 with the majority arriving from the Philippines.